POSTMODERN ENCOUNTERS

Postmodernism and Holocaust Denial

Robert Eaglestone

Series editor: Richard Appignanesi

ICON BOOKS UK

TOTEM BOOKS USA

Published in the UK in 2001
by Icon Books Ltd., Grange Road,
Duxford, Cambridge CB2 4QF
E-mail: info@iconbooks.co.uk
www.iconbooks.co.uk

Published in the USA in 2001
by Totem Books
Inquiries to: Icon Books Ltd.,
Grange Road, Duxford,
Cambridge CB2 4QF, UK

Sold in the UK, Europe, South Africa
and Asia by Faber and Faber Ltd.,
3 Queen Square, London WC1N 3AU
or their agents

Distributed to the trade in the USA by
National Book Network Inc.,
4720 Boston Way, Lanham,
Maryland 20706

Distributed in the UK, Europe,
South Africa and Asia by
Macmillan Distribution Ltd.,
Houndmills, Basingstoke RG21 6XS

Distributed in Canada by
Penguin Books Canada,
10 Alcorn Avenue, Suite 300,
Toronto, Ontario M4V 3B2

Published in Australia in 2001
by Allen & Unwin Pty. Ltd.,
83 Alexander Street,
Crows Nest, NSW 2065

Library of Congress catalog
card number applied for

Series editor: Richard Appignanesi

ISBN 1 84046 234 5

Typesetting by Wayzgoose

Printed and bound in the UK by
Cox & Wyman Ltd., Reading

Introduction: Trials and Genres

The charges which I have found to be substantially true include the charges that Irving has for his own ideological reasons persistently and deliberately misrepresented and manipulated historical evidence; that for the same reasons he has portrayed Hitler in an unwarrantedly favourable light, principally in relation to his attitude towards and responsibility for the treatment of the Jews; that he is an active Holocaust denier; that he is anti-Semitic and racist and that he associates with right wing extremists who promote neo-Nazism.

(*Judgement*, 13.167)[1]

Accuracy and clarity are important for all intellectual discussions. Discussions about the Holocaust, whether historical or philosophical, are no exception. The constellation of ideas described as postmodernism is often accused of being neither accurate nor clear. So, in order to anchor this discussion of postmodernism and Holocaust denial, I am going to concentrate on one particular, concrete, high-profile incident.

In the spring of 2000, the UK press was full of stories about a court case that ran from 11 January to 11 April: they called it 'The Irving Trial'. This name was inaccurate. Although trying 'to give the impression he was being sued and was the defendant in the case',[2] David Irving himself had brought libel charges against an American academic, Deborah Lipstadt, who had discussed him in her book *Denying the Holocaust: The Growing Assault on Truth and Memory*. If anyone, it was Lipstadt who was on trial. Irving argued that Lipstadt had 'vandalised [his] legitimacy as an historian' and had ruined his reputation by accusing him of being a Nazi apologist who distorted facts and manipulated documents. For Irving – and for the Judge, Mr. Justice Gray – the accusation that he was a bad historian was at the core of the case.

The misnaming of the trial is one of its lessons: a postmodern lesson about types or, more technically, *genres* of writing and their rules. News is a genre – it needs a 'story'. Covering the trial, journalists followed the old adage: 'dog bites man, no story: man bites dog, story'. There's no story, no surprise, in 'Jewish American academic attacks anti-Semitic Holocaust deniers'. In contrast, 'non-Jewish English historian denies Holocaust' has 'reader appeal'. Combining this with his skilful milking of press attention – he 'loved being the star of the show he himself had set in motion in Court 73 and revelled in the newspaper and television coverage' – the anti-Semitic and racist Irving got pages and pages of newsprint and airtime in the UK.[3] Photos of Irving, not Lipstadt, were on the front pages on the day after the judgement. Lipstadt didn't let Irving cross-examine her and turned down requests for interviews. With only a few exceptions, the press didn't bother explaining why she turned down interviews and spent hardly any time covering her arguments. Reading just the first page of *Denying the Holocaust* makes her reasons for both these decisions clear.

In other more important ways, the question of understanding and combating Holocaust denial is intimately tied up with ideas about genre and ideas about what history is. Outside the court, the issue raised questions about the role and scope of historians and the works of history they produce. As the newspapers said, but in a different sense, history was on trial here. And because the history under discussion was about the Holocaust, the event Elie Wiesel calls the 'black hole of history', it demanded to be approached seriously and soberly.[4]

Many who fight Holocaust denial, and many historians in general, put postmodernism, deconstruction or 'cultural relativism' together and find them threatening. Some suggest that these sorts of ideas, in fact, lead to Holocaust denial. Sometimes, for example, they point to the fact that the German philosopher Martin Heidegger (1889–1976), an influence on postmodernism, was a Nazi. That Holocaust denial happens at all is often posited as a 'knockdown' argument against postmodernism. The authors of *Telling the Truth about History* argue that 'cultural relativism had reached its limits in the death camps' and so seem to be drawing a parallel between contemporary postmodern thinkers and the Nazis.[5] (Has any group been *less* culturally relativist than the Nazis?) Richard Evans, one of the most significant contemporary historians of Germany and the defence's chief expert at the trial, wrote that postmodernist history 'demeans the dead'.[6] Lipstadt herself, although she acknowledges that postmodernists are not deniers or sympathetic to deniers, argues that:

[T]*he 'climate' these sort*[s] *of ideas create is of no less importance than the specific truth they attack . . . It is a climate that fosters deconstructionist history at its worst. No fact, no event, and no aspect of history has any fixed meaning or content. Any truth can be retold. Any fact can be recast. There is no ultimate historical reality . . . Holocaust denial is part of this phenomenon.*[7]

I want to argue that these accusations are, in the main, misplaced. Generally, I believe that postmodernism is a response to the Holocaust, questioning to its very core the culture that made it possible. But more than this, I want to argue here that the questions postmodernism asks of history and historians are very strong weapons in the fight against Holocaust denial. These questions are ways we can strip the masks of 'impartiality' and 'historical objectivity' from deniers to reveal denial for what it really is.

What is Denial?

Bluntly, Holocaust denial is the claim that the murder of approximately six million Jews in the Nazi genocide during the Second World War did not happen. Those who study denial attempt to divide deniers into 'hard' and 'soft' categories. 'Hard' deniers claim, for example, that the whole genocide is a hoax, concocted after the war. 'Soft' deniers claim, for example, that Jews were imprisoned in camps but died in limited numbers as a result of illness and other wartime deprivations, or that the genocide was not the result of a systematic Nazi policy, but the work of extremist Nazis elements (the idea of *extremist* Nazis – implying moderate Nazis – is an odd one, of course). However, these distinctions are rarely fixed, as they demand too much consistency from the world of bigotry and false argument that these people inhabit. Deniers find it hard to keep their stories straight and, when challenged, change their approaches, alter their theories and shift their emphasis. David Irving, for example, changed from a 'soft' denier to a 'hard' denier after reading a totally flawed and denier-motivated report on the gas chambers: a report that the distinguished Holocaust historian Robert Jan Van Pelt dismissed during the trial as 'scientific garbage' (see *Judgement*, 7.113–117). Van Pelt discusses and easily demolishes the changing stories and bizarre theories that have been offered by deniers about the Auschwitz gas chambers in his short book, *The Science of Holocaust Research and the Art of Holocaust Denial*.

However, more or less all the deniers in Europe and North America have a number of things in common. First, they are always anti-Semitic. So much so, in fact, that Holocaust denial can most simply and clearly be understood as a form of anti-Semitism: a post-war version of the forged anti-Semitic key text, *The Protocols of the Elders of Zion*.[8] Second, these deniers almost always support neo-fascist parties or sects. They seem to believe that if the Holocaust is 'removed' from the equation, if the Nazis are acquitted, if fascism is exonerated of these terrible deeds, people will somehow find their murderous and evil creeds of hate convincing. Third, and I will return to this, European and North American deniers are almost always racist, believing in both racist categories (that is, that people are defined in their very being by a pseudoscientific, un-historical and unhistoricised concept of race) and in the superiority of 'the Aryan race'. Finally, it is very hard to argue with deniers. Like all con-spiracy theorists, they always find new ways of explaining away the consensus of historians. For them, denying the Holocaust is not like establish-ing a historical datum, like how many ships fought at the Battle of Trafalgar or how many women died in childbirth in New York in 1905. For them – the self-selected arch-doubters – the non-existence of the genocide is beyond question, like an article of faith. Denying the Holocaust is a cornerstone for their anti-Semitic, racist and fascist beliefs.

In the last twenty years or so, deniers have developed new strategies to convey their mes-sage. Analysing the history of denial from its roots in pre-war anti-Semitism to the present day, Lipstadt's book is particularly acute about these changing strategies. Lipstadt explores in detail several of the different approaches deniers have taken. Deniers use tricks to get publicity. Here is one example, not covered by Lipstadt (although she does discuss this particular denier's other approaches). One denier wrote a book claiming that flying saucers were Axis secret weapons. In a phone conversation with Frank Miele, who was writing a piece on Holocaust denial for *Skeptic* magazine, the denier revealed that this was simply a ruse:

I realised that North Americans were not interested in being educated. They want to be entertained. The book was for fun. With a picture of the Führer on the cover and flying saucers coming out of Antarctica it was a chance to get on radio and TV talk shows. For about 15 minutes of an hour program I'd talk about that esoteric stuff. Then . . . that was my chance to talk about what I wanted to talk about.[9]

The 'wacky' title gave him the chance to broadcast his anti-Semitic Holocaust denial on Network TV, with the tacit support of Network broadcasters, who might not give airtime to a more 'typical', upfront denier.

However, this sort of pretence is minor, compared to the real threat Lipstadt analyses. She points out that, in recent years, deniers have tried to make their work look and sound like the work of professional historians engaged in an intellectual debate. To combat people like these, who she considers the main danger, Lipstadt writes that *'above all, it is essential to expose the illusion of reasoned inquiry that conceals their extremist view'*.[10] Lipstadt uses two broad 'pincers' to expose them. The first is to point out that the idea of a debate over the existence of the Holocaust is simply a sham. The second is to argue that there is a difference between what historians do and what Holocaust deniers do: between history and denial. These two strategies give the book its polemical tone and contentious edge.

Sham debates

On the first page of *Denying the Holocaust*, Lipstadt tells a story that serves as a leitmotif for her whole book.

The producer was incredulous. She found it hard to believe that I was turning down an opportunity to appear on her nationally televised show: 'But you are writing a book on this topic. It will be great publicity'. I repeatedly explained that I would not participate in a debate with a Holocaust denier. The existence of the Holocaust was not a matter of debate . . . I would not appear with them . . . To do so would give them a legitimacy and a stature they in no way deserve . . . [I]n one last attempt to get me to change my mind, she asked me a question: 'I certainly don't agree with them, but don't you think our viewers should hear the other side?'

The point is that there simply is no debate in any meaningful sense, no 'other side' about the existence of the Holocaust. Reasonable and responsible people don't have this debate, not least because, for the Holocaust, the 'evidence is over-whelming' (*Judgement*, 7.7). An expert on French denial, Pierre Vidal-Naquet, asks if an astronomer would discuss things with an astrologer, 'or with a person who claims that the moon is made of green cheese?'.[11] There are debates about the Holocaust, of course: history is not set in stone. For example, historians debate over how and why the murders took place when they did and how the Nazi hierarchy organised them; philo-sophers and theologians discuss the implications of the Holocaust; experts in cultural studies dis-cuss questions of memorialisation, and so on. There is no shortage of debates involving the Holocaust. But there is no debate over its *exis-tence*. Those who assert that there is such a debate, like the Nazi UFOs denier, are doing so to get 'airtime' and to make themselves seem more serious. This is why Lipstadt refused to give interviews: talking to them as if they were reason-able people gives credence to deniers.[12]

Imagine: what sort of person would appear on national TV to argue that you and your family are vermin? Why? Would you go on and argue that you weren't? Against a point of view like that, neither unprejudiced nor likely to be convinced by argument, how would you prove you weren't? What would that achieve, apart from a 'contentious' debate? What 'genre' of TV would it be? Serious documentary? Or just high-octane entertainment? Who would benefit? You? The TV company? The people taken seriously enough to go on TV with the original accusation? The audience?

The penultimate chapter of *Denying the Holocaust* is a case study of the 'sham debate' strategy. Entitled 'The Battle for the Campus', it describes how, in the early 1990s, a denier placed advertisements or opinion-editorial pieces denying the Holocaust in a number of US university newspapers. From his point of view, this was a win/win situation. If the pieces went in, his noxious ideas spread and the claim that this was 'the other side' of the story was made, giving credit to this sham debate. If they were refused, he got to make a fuss, claiming that he was being censored and that his constitutional right to free speech was being silenced by sinister Jewish interests and 'anti-freedom' elements (more anti-Semitism, of course). In fact, Lipstadt argues that this appeal to the US Constitution is a 'failure to understand the true implications of the First Amendment'.[13] Some papers refused publication: more did not. Some condemned the ads from their editorials. The series of events left Lipstadt pessimistic: students who had read, or even heard of the 'controversy', 'may have walked away . . . convinced that there are two sides to this debate: the "revisionists" and the "establishment historians" . . . That is the most frightening aspect of this entire matter'.[14]

Significantly, these events coincided with what was called 'the culture wars' on American campuses and in American intellectual life. To sum up a complex series of arguments, with rights and wrongs on both sides, the 'culture wars' debates, ostensibly over education, were actually about the whole structure of American society. On one side were more traditional, conservative ideas, described most famously in Allan Bloom's 1987 *The Closing of the American Mind* and echoed by others, such as the journalist Dinesh D'Souza.

On the other was a fissiparous grouping of those with more radical and often leftist ideas about issues such as race, gender and sexuality. Also on this side, often uneasily, were many 'postmodern' and deconstructive critics and writers. The debates over the mostly meaningless label of 'political correctness' were tied up in this, too.

These 'campus deniers' used the 'culture wars' and discussions of 'PC' as a way in. Since the 'PC' position was that the Holocaust had happened, they suggested that to attack this belief was daring, challenging and radical, just like the risqué US talk show, 'Politically Incorrect', seemed to be. Anti-Semitism and race hatred, 'correctly cast and properly camouflaged', were trying to claim the pseudo-rebellious kudos of being 'politically incorrect'.[15] Of course, those pilloried for 'being PC' fought these hatreds just as Lipstadt fights them in her book. Peter Novick suggests that Lipstadt saw the success of this denial campaign as 'evidence of the strength of postmodernism and deconstructionism in the Universities' and, as a 'front' in the culture war, this was a 'theme picked up by conservative commentators'.[16] In contrast, Novick suggests that the real influences on the editors were the much less contentious liberal thinkers Thomas Jefferson and John Stuart Mill. The deniers' trick here was to 'piggyback' in on a real debate. Denial was not and is not a symptom of the intellectual substance of the 'culture wars' or debates over 'PC', despite the fact that the conservative side seemed to think it was. It is important to differentiate, as Lipstadt does, between real debates and sham debates. As I will argue below, postmodernism excludes denial as reasonable debate. That said, of course, deniers will use any trick they can to broadcast their views, and presumably enjoy the dissension sown amongst all those people of good will opposing them. And posing as conservative historians is one of their strongest tricks.

Deniers posing as historians

The false idea of an 'other side of a debate' relies on there seeming to be 'serious people' involved in this debate. This is the second target of Lipstadt's book. Part of the camouflage that deniers use is the appearance of 'reasoned historical inquiry'.

One of the most significant examples is The Institute of Historical Review in California. It sounds like a research centre in an established university: it produces a journal, complete with scholarly footnotes and apparatus, holds conferences and so on. It is, however, an organisation dedicated to Holocaust denial.

But David Irving was much more significant. As one leading professor of Jewish history, David Cesarani, pointed out, and as *The Guardian* declared, he was 'the Holocaust deniers' best shot'.[17] Irving began writing in the early 1960s: his books, generally published by reputable publishers, cover the events of the Second World War and, in part because he didn't talk about Nazi flying saucers, he was seen by many as a serious historian. It was this reputation as a historian that was at the centre of the case. If he was credible as a historian, his findings, however 'controversial', would stand as history to be debated and discussed. If he was not a credible or reasonable historian, his work – and he – would fall. This means that the case was also about what history is and what historians do.

In 1990, Irving gave a speech to the Institute of
Historical Review, called 'Battleship Auschwitz'.
It ended, in the pseudo-heroic rhetoric typical of
deniers, in a rather creepy parody of British and
American naval war films: he commanded 'Sink
the Auschwitz!'.[18] Like the deniers who have had
high-profile trials in Canada and Germany, Irving
was setting out to encounter his enemies on the
seas that suited him best. A leading lawyer wrote
that 'English libel law has notorious draconian
features reflecting its origins in the seventeenth-
century Court of Star Chamber. It puts the burden on the publisher to prove the truth of his [*sic*]
allegations'.[19] English libel law takes the side of
the plaintiff and assumes the libellous allegations
to be false until substantially justified. Addition-
ally, in recent high-profile cases in the UK, judge-
ments have usually gone with the plaintiff. Irving
was presumably hoping that a debate in a law
court would confirm his standing as a historian
and so his 'findings'. By doing this he would validate some of the claims of Holocaust deniers. If it
didn't, he still had the chance to broadcast his
views: another denier's win/win situation. This

was why he forced a confrontation by suing Lipstadt and Penguin. Penguin was not 'out for Irving's blood', as some suggested (rather distastefully, given the subject matter).[20] Irving wanted to use a court of law as a tool for Holocaust denial. Both Lipstadt and her publishers deserve to be congratulated for standing up to this. Irving lost spectacularly, leaving his reputation in tatters.

But the court case did more than just finish off Irving's reputation and damage – let's hope irreparably – Holocaust denial. It also raised questions about the nature of history itself.

The Nature of History

Despite their very great differences, Irving and Lipstadt have something in common. They share one particular understanding of what history actually is: they have what might be called a traditional empiricist view. And it is precisely this view that postmodernism questions. As I have suggested, many historians and cultural commentators are profoundly worried by this, especially in relation to the Holocaust. However, I aim to show that these questions are important and extremely useful tools with which to fight denial.

To adapt a metaphor from Mary Midgley, the British philosopher of science, history is like a computer. Usually we send e-mails, surf the net or word process, without a thought for the software that supports these applications. However, when the computer crashes or becomes infected with a virus, we need to look below the 'desktop' and into the complexities and details of the software. When history 'crashes' or becomes infected, what we take for granted – principally, I suggest, the 'objectivity' of history – has to be closely examined and perhaps 'debugged'. And this is what postmodernism offers to history.

History, as we understand it, has a history. It was constructed as a particular form of knowledge and way of doing things. As there are a number of excellent studies of this, I will only offer here a very short summary.[21] What we generally understand to be 'history' today, a fully established subject separate from other disciplines, stems from the work of Otto Von Ranke, a nineteenth-century German historian. The way of studying the past that he established spread over the Western world and is basically what both Lipstadt and Irving mean by 'history'. From Ranke and his followers, too, comes the discipline's desire to be a 'science of the past': to explain the past by representing it. This has perhaps three key features. First, it aims to recreate the past by representing (re-presenting), in Ranke's famous phrase, *wie es eigentlich gewesen*, 'what actually happened'. (Richard Evans suggests a better translation: 'how it actually was', but the sense remains fairly similar.[22]) Second, it demands that the historian must be objective and ignore his or her location in the world. Third, it demands that the historian follows an empirical method and, passive in the face of the facts, simply marshals the evidence.

However, many people – not just post-modernists – have questioned these ideas. These questions can be put into three broad categories: questions about epistemology or *how* we know about the past; questions about *who* is creating the history; and questions about the *nature of language and writing* itself. The outcome of these questions seems to disrupt traditional and some-times naïve notions of history.

How we study the past: knowing and telling

Epistemology is the branch of philosophy that deals with how we know things. When I ask you not 'if', but '*how*' you know that it is raining out-side, this is an epistemological question. In rela-tion to the past, epistemology explores how we can claim to know historical facts. To any his-torian, this presents a number of substantial, but often unexamined, problems.

First, no historian's account can cover the bulk of the past. The fact that there is so much of it means that anything like a full account is simply impossible. This is the novelistic insight of the English eighteenth-century writer Laurence Sterne's *Tristram Shandy*: no matter how fast Tristram writes he can never describe his whole life. Most – if not nearly all – information is not recorded (what colour socks did your neighbour wear last week? Last year? Did his great grandfather wear?) or is evanescent, here then gone (how many people on that street now, this second? Did you take a photo? What do they think about this morning's main news story?).

Second, the past is not an account, but events, responses and situations that have, well, passed. We can't judge the accuracy of an account of the past by going back to it, the way we might be able to judge the accuracy of a map of a city by walking around the area it is supposed to represent. In fact, most of us judge the accuracy of one historian's accounts by comparing them to another historian's accounts. This is rather like checking yesterday's events by comparing different newspapers from today. Other historians can check archival sources: rather like seeing if, as a journalist reported, the thief's footprint is still there the next morning. But neither of these is the same as checking the account against the actual event, which is impossible as the past has gone forever.

Third, events happen one way – forwards – but are learnt about and written about in another – backwards. History is retrospective. David Lowenthal cites an essay from 1964: 'time is foreshortened, details selected and highlighted, action concentrated, relations simplified not to deliberately alter . . . the events but to . . . give them meaning'.[23] History is made up of 'significant events'. Of course, not all the historical knowledge a historian has is written down, but the events of the past are always seen, explained and represented retrospectively.

So, knowledge about the past is edited, unverifiable by simple comparison, and studied backwards. This means that there is a difference between the past (the events that have now gone, are no longer actually present, however strong our memories of them) and history. History is not the recreation of the past as it actually was. It is the name for the *stories we tell about the past*. It is a type or *genre* of story. This is not to say that any particular account isn't true, but that the 'truth of the past' cannot be established in the same sort of way that the truth of the statement 'it is now raining outside' can be. How we know about the past is not straightforward and all historians know this.

Who is creating the history?
This is another issue that questions the traditional understanding of history. It is often misunder-

stood in the following way: people sometimes claim that 'men write different history from women, white people write different history from black people' and so on. This is not necessarily the case. What *is* the case is that historians of different nationalities, races, sexes, sexualities and so on, often have different aims and interests that stem from who they are: these different interests will cause them to look at different things in different ways. Predictably, for example, 'Women's history' and 'Black history' were ignored for much of the twentieth century, as, more or less, white men were interested in the events they took to be centrally important. However, there is nothing in principle to stop a man writing a fascinating and detailed history of women in nineteenth-century America, or a black person writing the history of almost all-white Ireland. Suggesting that the person's identity is the same as their method is a mistake, albeit an easily made one. (This is not to say that the 'location' of a historian isn't important. Like most people, historians and academics in general want to be successful, to have good careers, to be respected and so on, and this affects their interests: in this light Lipstadt's refusal to appear on national TV – with the money and kudos that would entail – is even more principled!) What is crucial is not, as it were, the historian's genes, but *what* the historian chooses to focus on, *how* they choose to do it and finally, in turn, what those choices themselves depend on.

I have already argued that there is just too much of the past to 'simply' recreate it 'as it happened'. Historians choose what to focus on. For example, in his masterpiece *The Destruction of the European Jews*, the great Holocaust historian Raul Hilberg chose to focus on the victims of the Holocaust and, in general, the administrative and bureaucratic means of their murder: the work of 'desk killers' like Eichmann. More recently, in his book *Ordinary Men*, Christopher Browning chose to focus on the perpetrators by looking in detail at the day-to-day genocidal activities in occupied Poland of one particular group of Germans – Reserve Police Battalion 101 – 'who were quite literally saturated in the blood of victims at point-blank range'.[24] (*Pause: writing and reading about the Holocaust is, and ought to be, distress-*

ing: however, sometimes, for me at least, it can happen that the nature of the subject is eclipsed for a moment by the heat of writing and debate. This is wrong. So, compare: think about getting blood on your clothes from a nosebleed: think how much, much more blood – the blood of the victims – would 'saturate with blood' a thick military uniform. On one day. And the killings, of all sorts, lasted years. This so-called 'comparison' is not even really a comparison.) These books, Hilberg's and Browning's, offer different, but linked, histories of the past.

But these choices are more than just a question of where the camera is pointed. They also rely, to extend this metaphor, on what *sort* of camera is used. Each historian takes for granted some key concepts. These ideas will vary with each approach: for a Marxist historian, concepts like 'base and superstructure' or 'class' will structure his or her view and orient his or her historical knowledge; a more conservative historian, believing that the future is dark and the present burdensome, will take for granted the inevitably imperfect make-up of human nature; a historian influenced by the French thinker Michel Foucault (1926–84) will have ideas about 'the body', 'genealogy' and 'rupture' at the front of his or her mind; a liberal, believing that 'from the crooked timber of humanity no straight thing can ever be made' will praise tolerance and look askance at the intolerant; for those of the influential Annalist school, wider issues of geography or economics will be central, and so on. These are enormous differences of perspective and approach and they lead to differences of interpretation and explanation. As a result, history – the genre of stories about the past – is never *just* stories. Implicitly or explicitly, any particular history also embodies a methodology or philosophy of history. More than being about the past, any history is also an example of how that methodology works. Perhaps different ways of writing history might correspond to different 'sub-genres' of history.

An example of this, again drawn from Holocaust history, is the conflict of views between Christopher Browning and Daniel Jonah Goldhagen. Browning aims 'to explain why ordinary men – shaped by a culture that had its own particularities but was nonetheless within the mainstream of Western, Christian and Enlightenment tradition – under specific circumstances willingly carried out the most extreme genocide in human history'.[25] As his title suggests, his study looks at the *Ordinary Men* who murdered Jews. As a basically liberal historian looking at recorded activities, Browning's study reveals how most of these seemingly average men were transformed into killers. He argues that indoctrination, peer pressure, wartime Nazi propaganda and the very nature of the Second World War led to this transformation. While in no way equating these murderous perpetrators with their innocent victims, he points out how they were manipulated by the structure of the Nazi regime. He draws a guarded parallel with the famous 1960s 'obedience to authority' experiments of Stanley Milgram, in which scientists persuaded volunteers to 'electrocute' fake subjects in a laboratory.

Goldhagen, looking mostly at the same records and archives, had a different approach: his disagreement with Browning and his own conclusion are clearly signified in his title, *Hitler's*

Willing Executioners: Ordinary Germans and the Holocaust. Goldhagen wants to answer the question: 'what was the structure of beliefs and values that made a genocidal onslaught against the Jews intelligible and sensible to the ordinary Germans who became perpetrators?'[26] Seemingly unlike Browning, Goldhagen is explicitly interested in the ideas and mindsets that lead to people's actions: not 'structural' reasons, but what he calls the 'ideational causes of social action'.[27] Although he acknowledges that the 'incentive structure' (for example, indoctrination, fear of punishment or hope for official or social reward) is important, he believes that this alone cannot cause people to act but works 'in conjunction with the cognitive and value structures' already in place in an individual.[28] This, he argues, is the difference between his and other explanations of the Holocaust, 'generated either in a laboratory' (a pop at Browning's use of Milgram's results) or 'deduced from some philosophical or theoretical system'.[29] (Goldhagen's approach is 'theoretical' too, of course: he uses, in part, the 'thick description' approach, discussed by the anthropologist Clifford Geertz.) Goldhagen's conclusion? Germany, unlike other European countries, had a 'dominant cultural thread' of 'eliminationist anti-Semitism'.[30] The mindset of ordinary Germans was used to – and supported – the idea of the utter annihilation of the Jews. Thus, unlike Browning's killers, manipulated into genocide, Goldhagen argues that Germans in general and the killers specifically were willing accomplices, motivated by a thoroughgoing and deep-seated hatred of the Jews. As Browning says in his generous but critical account of Goldhagen, it is, of course, not unusual 'for different scholars to ask different questions of, apply different methodologies to, and derive different interpretations from the same sources'.[31] The differences between these two accounts stem from wide differences in perspective and approach; differences, in fact, in their philosophy of history.

However, and even more importantly, differences in perspective, in methodology and in the philosophy of history, such as the differences between Goldhagen and Browning, stem from 'extra-historical' ideas. That is, such differences don't just stem from a historian's belief about the past, but from their wider beliefs about the world – their philosophical 'worldview' – however clearly or indistinctly it is worked out. A Marxist historian is a Marxist because he or she believes that Marxism is the best way to bring about social justice; liberal historians believe that tolerance is the greatest virtue; a conservative believes that traditions can teach us how to live best, and so on. It is because of this that history is always history for a particular reason which supports, without necessarily stating it explicitly, a certain cause or worldview. So, not only is all history shaped by a methodology or philosophy of history, but it is also directed, unavoidably, by an implicit or explicit worldview, too. History is always *history from* a certain worldview.

This is why, in the main, postmodernists argue that 'pure', 'neutral' or 'objective' history is impossible. Not because one can only tell the story of one's own identity (e.g. as a white man), but because each history, each story about the past, evolves from the historian's focus, the historian's methodology and philosophy of history, which is in turn shaped by the historian's ideas, clear or fuzzy, about life and the world: their worldview. And there is no such thing as an objective philosophy or worldview – if there were, everybody would share it, and philosophers would stop arguing. (It was hoped that science would prove to be an 'objective philosophy' and indeed, science tells us a great deal. Carbon dating gives us approximate dates for excavated bodies and so on: but science can't tell us what actions will result in social justice, whether human nature exists or, if it does, whether it can be improved. Science can't tell us what poor women in London in 1789 thought about the French Revolution. Nor can science, I suspect, tell us how to make ethically good decisions.) Of course, some of these points have been raised before. Herodotus, often heralded as the 'father of history', knew he was writing from a position. But postmodernism, as I suggest below, makes these points again, in new and urgent ways.

The nature of language and writing

So far, I have argued that history is a genre that writes and learns retrospectively about the past, selecting key meaningful events. I have stated that it is impossible to verify an account about the past by going back to the past (the way you can verify the weather *right now* by stepping outside). Accounts are shaped by the historian's methodology and this, in turn, relies on their worldview. This means that history is not recreation of the past 'as it really was', but the name we give to the genre of stories we tell about the past. It is because of this that Hayden White, an influential thinker on the nature of history, argues that a historical work is 'a narrative prose discourse that purports to be a model, or icon, of past structures and processes in the interests of explaining what they were by representing them'.[32] This is absolutely not to say that events didn't happen or are 'made up' (or made to disappear), but that unlike the novelist:

. . . the historian confronts a veritable chaos of events already constituted, out of which he [sic]

must choose the elements of the story he [sic]
would tell. He [sic] *makes his* [sic] *story by including some events and excluding others, by stressing
some and subordinating others. This process . . . is
carried out in the interest of constituting a story of
a particular kind. That is to say, he* [sic] *'emplots'
his* [sic] *story.*[33]

Writing meaningfully about the past is, and can
only be, the 'emplotment' of events of the past
into certain types of story.

In his major study, *Metahistory*, White outlines
the interactions between what he calls the 'model
of ideological implication' (roughly, what I called
the worldview), the mode of argument (roughly,
the sort of 'camera' or methodology used) and
'mode of emplotment' – what sort of story it is.
He identifies four 'modes' of story: romantic,
tragic, comic and satiric. I am not going to discuss these in detail, but mention them in order to
show that, because of the nature of writing and
narrating itself, a particular history is not 'objective'. It will always be in a mode of 'emplotment':
not necessarily one of the forms from White's list,

but in the form of a story of some sort. Even 'chronicle history', made up of simple lists of events, is like this. A king is crowned, fights invaders and dies: a simple story, of course, but a story nonetheless. This also displays the characteristics of history I discussed above, through, for example, the events chosen – the death of a king is chosen over the death of a queen or a shepherd. The very need to keep a chronicle reflects a wider worldview showing the chronicler's desire to impose his or her values, a society that wants or needs to pass down information, and so on.

More than just 'emplotted', each history is also constructed as a narrative *for* an audience. Quite rightly, history books for students at school aged 12 are different from those written with a specialised, highly informed and critical audience in mind, and these in turn differ from books written for the general reader. This too means that works of history cannot be 'objective', as the choices made about level of detail, for example, don't reflect an objective past but putative readers: all history is *history for* an audience. Furthermore, any work of history also has to be written in a certain style.

Traditionally, history is written in the third person, in the style favoured by realist novelists. 'The advantage of third person narration', writes the eminent critic Frank Kermode, 'is that it is the mode which best produces the illusion of pure reference. But it is an illusion, the effect of a rhetorical device'.[34] That is, the key feature of this 'realist' style is to give the impression that it is not really a style at all, but a transparent window (or 'reference') to the world beyond – in the past or in fiction. Despite this impression, the 'realist style' is one choice from many different styles of writing, and one chosen with a reason: as the old joke has it, once you can fake sincerity, you can fake anything.

The central point of all these arguments is that a history text is not a clear window to the past: it is not really objective at all. Instead, history books are texts about the past: they stand in for, or are perhaps analogous to, the absent and unrecoverable past. 'Pure', 'neutral' or 'objective' history is impossible. Historical knowledge is produced, and history books are written, as a genre. And it is this concept of 'history as genre' that was central to the Lipstadt–Irving case.

The Rules of Genres

Genres of writing and types of knowledge have rules or 'generic conventions'. There are, of course, many genres of text, normally divided by content. In fiction, it's easy to spot genres such as the thriller, romance and science fiction. While novels are divided by content, works of history are almost always divided up chronologically and geographically, although there are sub-genres such as 'Women's history', 'Oral history' and 'Military history'. But more important than where the books go in a bookshop are the generic conventions that structure the works. Generic conventions are parts of plot or style that are special to that genre: all texts, not just novels, have generic rules. These rules are present in the content: you expect a dashing hero in a romantic novel; you expect to read about grain production in economic history, troop movements in military history; we all expect a cookbook to be about cooking food. The conventions are also present in the style: hard-boiled detective stories have a terse style; academic histories have long sentences and lots of footnotes; cookbooks have lists of ingredients.

The rules of a particular genre don't just set up the parameters, however: they actually *construct* that text. After all, what is a detective thriller without a detective or a cookbook without recipes? Genres are not pigeonholes into which academics and bookshop owners put books: they are the rules underlying the books themselves. To write anything is to be part of a genre, to follow (and sometimes to bend slightly or to adapt) generic rules. Some of these rules matter very little (it doesn't matter whether the heroic cowboy has a black or a white hat), some of them are absolutely central and vital. The genre of history has a number of central rules. The historian Geoffrey Elton, distinctly unpostmodern and pro-Rankean, was aware of this. He argued that the 'conditions of professional competence and integrity' for historical work were only guaranteed by a professional training as a historian.[35] This can be read as arguing that the generic conventions that are central to history are taught implicitly through this arduous, professional training, and only once this has taken place – only once the historian knows the rules – is the history any good.

Generic conventions or rules are, then, extremely important for history. If 'objectivity' is a myth, these conventions offer the idea of the 'reasonable historian' and a way of understanding what the genre of history is.

Much in law depends on assessments of what a 'reasonable person' would expect or think. Exactly what the 'reasonable person' believes in every case is hard to pin down – after all, you'd need a list of everything from aardvarks to zebras to do the concept full justice – but it is part of the reason for 'trial by jury' by one's peers. This 'reasonable person' concept plays a crucial part in professional negligence cases. When deciding whether a defendant has met the standard of care in medical negligence cases, courts apply the 'Bolam test', named for the *Bolam v. Friern Hospital Management Committee* case of 1957: a 'doctor is not guilty of negligence if he has acted in accordance with a practice accepted as proper by a responsible body of medical men [*sic*] skilled in that particular art'. Not all doctors have to agree that the practice in question is the only practice, but only that it is a recognised, responsible one. The Bolam test, or versions of it, has been accepted outside medical cases too: anywhere, in fact, that issues of negligence and the duty of care arise. Among those who write history, there is the same sort of idea in a more limited spectrum: the idea of a 'reasonable historian'.

The idea of the 'reasonable historian' stems from two things. First, it comes from the tradition that – like scientists – all historians share a huge project, all working to illuminate the past, as nuclear physicists work to illuminate the nature of the atom. Historians (although it might not seem like it) form a community that, like all communities, is constructed and defined by implicit or explicit adherence to certain *conventions* (the word originally means 'coming together'). Second, the idea of a 'reasonable historian' means that each historian has followed a recognised mode of argument, or argued for and defended the way they have chosen to work: thus, they are 'reasonable' in that they have a reasoned method. Both of these can be seen as ways in which historians define and police the genre of history by a circular definition that relies on generic conventions. A 'reasonable historian' is somebody who writes according to the generic conventions that define history: history is written in the light of the generic conventions that historians, usually implicitly, decide upon. What makes both a 'reasonable historian' and a work generically 'history' is an adherence to the appropriate generic conventions. (Although this might seem odd, there isn't anything strange about it. After all, a Society of Thriller Writers won't give its annual award to the author of a cookbook, and cookbooks don't usually contain white-knuckle car chases.) For reasons I have discussed above, a 'reasonable historian' is often, wrongly, thought of as being an 'objective historian'. And again, let me stress that this doesn't mean history isn't true: it just means that history texts are not transparent or objective and can't establish the truth in the same way as you can check the weather.

This concept of the 'reasonable historian' explains why controversies between historians are rarely about 'particular facts' and are so fierce. A historian seldom attacks another's knowledge of an archive: more often they attack the way they have chosen to approach history. Controversies are about the way history is done and what is 'reasonable'. As I have argued, this in turn relies on worldviews. So with Irving, the attack was not basically about what archives he had used, but *how* he had used them and so about his worldview. A reasonable historian is at least one that other historians can 'reason' with, even if there could be no final agreement. Of course, what defines 'reasonable' can change as new ideas and methods sweep across the historical community, just as new sub-genres of writing are created. But this takes time, happens slowly and with great debate. Feminist historians had to fight hard, and for a long time, before their different ways of being 'reasonable historians' became accepted, for example.

Despite changes, there are some conventions that have remained fairly stable. One of the most significant of these is the use of evidence. The support of argument from evidence is perhaps the central convention of the genre of history, and differentiates it most clearly from fiction. Just as scientists undertake experiments, historians use traces of the past in the present – for example, documents and oral statements – to support their arguments. Crudely, this is the demand that historical texts have sources: more technically, as Frank Kermode puts it, the genre of history needs 'metatextual announcements [that is, references to texts apart from itself], references to sources and authorities, assurance to the credibility of witnesses'.[36] People who don't follow this convention – say, by discussing UFOs without evidence – are simply not doing history.

But the 'evidence convention' is even stronger. Evidence has to be 'reliable' or 'testable'. This is best thought about as an analogue to 'scientific repeatability'. Basically, when a historian makes 'metatextual reference' by citing a piece of evidence (a letter, say), another historian needs to be able to find it and check it, just as scientists need to be able to repeat their colleague's experiments. The Lipstadt trial has an example of this. Studying Himmler's phone log, Irving argued that on 1 December 1941 Himmler telephoned an SS General to tell him that Jews were to 'stay where they are', thus portraying Himmler as saving Jews. Irving read 'Verwaltungsfuhrer der SS haben zu bleiben' (Administrative leaders of the SS have to stay) and mistook 'haben' for 'Juden' (thus: 'Administrative leaders of the SS. Jews to stay'). He ignored the lack of a full stop and the fact that 'Administrative leaders of the SS. Jews to stay' doesn't actually make sense. As the chief defence witness, Richard Evans checked the documents ('repeated the experiment') and found Irving's error. Evans argued that it was 'deliberately a perverse misreading' and it does seem an odd mistake for a man so keen on factual detail to make. Irving now admits that he misread 'haben'. This insistence on 'testability' is a central convention of the genre of history.

Another convention linked to this is the use of sources. An example: Irving wanted to claim that Hitler didn't know about the extermination of the Jews in Eastern Europe (a typical 'soft' denier claim). In his accounts, he cites a particular passage from Goebbels's diary: the 'Jews must get out of Europe. If need be, we must resort to the most brutal methods'. However, in addition to ignoring an array of other sources and documents, Irving has edited out a great deal of the passage. Crucial, according to Evans, is Irving's omission of Goebbels's description of Hitler as 'the persistent pioneer and spokesman of a radical solution' which, Evans argued, 'must indicate that Hitler was aware what was going on in the extermination camps in the East' (*Judgement*, 5.174, 5.175). The issue here is more complicated because it is obviously impossible for any historian to cite every source completely, and because each historian uses sources in the light of their own methodology and worldview. However, relying on the 'testability' of evidence and the idea of the 'reasonable historian', it is possible to see how far the generic conventions have been followed. A 'reasonable historian' doesn't make unreasonable edits from quotations.

Historical writing must also be consistent. Where a novelist, like Norman Mailer in the 'factional' *The Executioner's Song*, can mix evidence with speculation and invented ideas, a work of history must be consistent in the way it follows genre conventions. Where it doesn't (where more is speculation, for example), this has to be clearly signalled.

Another convention, as I have already suggested, is that historians generally write in the third person in a style recognised as 'realist'. Not writing in this style is frowned upon. Those who don't choose this style are not seen as historians. An example: Gitta Sereny has written a number of historical books, complete with scholarly apparatus, archival research and interviews. However, because her books are in the first person and are mostly concerned with what Goldhagen might call 'ideational causes of social action', she is described in Mr. Justice Gray's report, and in other places, as a 'journalist' (*Judgement*, 6.104). She uses the wrong style for the generic conventions.

In conclusion then, being a 'reasonable historian' and producing history means following the rules of the genre. I have discussed a handful of these above. These rules can be followed more or less well. Following these rules does not make texts more or less objective: objectivity is a fondly cherished myth. What it does is to make the works more or less historical, more or less of that genre of knowledge and of writing. Holocaust denial doesn't obey the rules of the genre. Therefore, Holocaust denial isn't part of the genre of history, but another genre, the genre of politics or of 'hate-speech'. What Irving was desperate to do was show that he was a valid historian, that he had followed the generic conventions and that his conclusions were, as a consequence, part of 'history'. In fact, he showed that he didn't follow the conventions and so his work was simply anti-Semitism.

Postmodernism, History and the Trial

To return to the 'computer' metaphor: we can only deal with the virus of Irving's claim to be a reasonable and objective historian, by looking deep into the software of history. The issues I have discussed are 'postmodern' for two reasons. One, because they are to do with the fact that history (separate from memory) is not the past objectively reconstructed, but texts constituted by generic rules that claim to represent the past. Two, and as a consequence of the first, because it is by thinking about and admitting that historical writing evolves from specific methodologies and worldviews, and is not 'objective work', that the link between denial and anti-Semitism, fascism and racism is made utterly explicit. (Other, 'unpostmodern' sorts of questions might include discussions of completeness of archival research, the reconciliation of data from different archives and so on: not 'software' questions as such, but important ones beyond the remit of this book.) As I suggested earlier, postmodernism has been much criticised because it can seem antithetical to history. Some writers, categorised as post-modern, have indeed written rather foolishly on history and no one should defend bad scholar-ship or lack of thought. However, I have suggested that postmodern questions are, in fact, neither 'pro' nor 'con' history as such. Rather, they seek to open up the processes by which history is done and the claims made for historical work. When the computer of history has become infected with a virus, it is no good just pressing the same keys that used to make it work: it has to be looked into in depth. If objectivity as an idea for history has broken down, it is no good repeatedly stating that history should be objective: the ideas that underlie history must be re-examined. Even Richard Evans, no friend of postmodernism, argues that it 'is right and proper that post-modernist theories and critics should force historians to rethink the categories and assumptions by which they work, and to justify the manner in which they pursue their discipline'.[37]

My argument has been very influenced by the work of the French philosopher Jean-François Lyotard.[38] Lyotard is a key figure for post-modernism and summarising his thought in detail is impossible in a book of this genre. As the author of *The Postmodern Condition*, he suggested that what made us 'postmodern' was the fact that we were 'incredulous about meta-narratives'.

For Lyotard, a metanarrative was a huge story that helped orient us in the world, that gave us direction and explained all the other narratives around us. Marxism is an example of a meta-narrative. For a Marxist, the dynamic of 'class struggle' and the materialist theory of Marx explain every event and human action. Another metanarrative would be 'Whig' liberalism or progress: the idea that the human race is getting better with each passing moment and will eventually become perfect. However, after all the changes in the last third of the twentieth century, he suggests that we are no longer able to trust any of these stories. We no longer believe them or that any one theory seems to explain everything. This is the 'climate' that Lipstadt thinks aids Holocaust denial.

Lyotard, like Lipstadt, was well aware that this sort of 'climate' raised problems for ethical and historical discussion. But rather than passing over it, and because, as a philosopher, he thought deeply about the Holocaust, he wrote *The Differend: Phrases in Dispute*. The book begins with an account of Holocaust denial and aims to show how the postmodern condition repudiates denial. The book is very complex, drawing on the history of philosophy, law, ethics, epistemology and history. One result of this complexity is that the different readings of it stress different aspects of the argument: usually the ethical argument is seen as most important. However, one of the key parts of the book is about precisely how, in post-modernity, after 'objectivity' has been revealed to be a comforting myth, facts and events in the past can be found to be truly represented.

Lyotard writes that reality 'is not "given" . . . it is the state of the referent (that about which one speaks) which results from the effectuation of establishment procedures defined by a unani-mously agreed upon protocol, and from the pos-sibility offered to anyone to recommence this effectuation as often as he or she wants'.[39] He spends much of the book working out in detail how to establish reality. He argues that we work in 'phrases': by this he means something like 'language-games', ways of talking and under-standing or, significantly, genres. Each type of phrase has different 'rules' and blind spots. For example, the phrase of naming gives a relation-ship to other phrases ('London' is in 'Britain', 'Hamlet' is 'Claudius's nephew'), but no actual location or solidity (where are they both? There was and is no 'actual' Hamlet). He argues that reality is established only when three sorts of phrases, three sorts of definition coincide: when reality is 'able to be signified, to be shown and to be named'.[40] With any item, to be signified is to be given a context in which it makes sense; to be shown is literally to be shown it; to be named is to be given a designation and identity that fixes it. To give an example: 'an agricultural implement, here, a spade' (signified, shown, named). Or 'a telephone log entry relevant to the murder of Jews, here is the text, made by Himmler' (signified, shown, named). None of these phrases can validate itself by itself: just being shown an object that you really couldn't identify several times wouldn't help you know what it is. Just being shown the diary entry isn't enough: it needs a name, context and meaning to become a 'historical fact'. All this means that, in order to establish the sort of 'historical reality' that Lipstadt wants, it is vitally important to know what sort of phrases or genre you are using, or are being used. Holocaust deniers, Lyotard argues, do not 'have a stake in establishing reality', do not 'accept the rules for forming and validating' statements: 'his [sic] goal is not to convince. The historian need not convince [a denier] if [the denier] is "playing" another genre of discourse, one in which conviction, or, obtaining a consensus over a defined reality is not at stake. Should the historian persist along this path, he [*sic*] will end up in the position of victim'.[41] Lipstadt was, indeed, the defendant in the case.

But what genres was Irving using? Not the genre of history. David Irving failed the generic conventions of history in many ways. The court found the following long list of accusations substantially justified: Irving 'distorts accurate historical evidence and information; misstates; misconstrues; misquotes; falsifies statistics; falsely attributes conclusions to reliable sources; manipulates documents; wrongfully quotes from books that directly contradict his arguments in such a manner as completely to distort their authors' objectives and while counting on the ignorance or indolence of the majority of readers not to realise this . . . wears blinkers and skews documents and misrepresents data in order to reach historically untenable conclusions specifically those that exonerate Hitler' (*Judgement*, 2.10).

But more than this, his worldview was an unreasonable one. He was judged to be an anti-Semite and a racist. These things prevented him doing 'reasonable history'. (This is the significance to the case of the poem, much discussed in the press, that he often sang to his daughter – 'I am a Baby Aryan/Not Jewish or Sectarian/I have no plans to marry an/Ape or Rastafarian' (*Judgement*, 9.6). Irving is a racist through and through and that worldview affects his historical writing.) The details of his 'history' showed that his methodology was wrong, which in turn showed that his worldview was and is profoundly flawed.

This means that, counter-intuitively, the point of all the historical testimony was *not* really to prove Irving *wrong* as a historian. It was to show that most of the time he wasn't really a historian at all, he was writing a different genre altogether, an anti-Semitic fascist diatribe. *Holocaust denial isn't bad history: it isn't any sort of history at all, and simply can't be discussed as if it is.*

This was the position argued by Richard Rampton, defending Lipstadt and Penguin (who is more aware of genre than lawyers?). He began his speech, echoing Richard Evan's report, by arguing 'Mr. Irving calls himself an historian. The truth is, however, that he is not an historian at all'. The defence's winning case rested on providing substantial examples of where Irving had failed the genre requirements of history. The judge, too, was aware of the utmost significance of 'genre' too. Throughout the judgement, Mr. Justice Gray is at pains to point out that a law court is not the 'court of history'. He states that his job is to 'evaluate the criticisms' of Irving's 'conduct as an historian in the light of the available historical evidence':

But it is not for me to form, still less to express, a judgement about what happened. That is a task for historians. It is important that those reading this judgement should bear well in mind the distinction between my judicial role in resolving the issues arising between these parties and the role of the historian seeking to provide an accurate narrative of past events.

(*Judgement*, 1.3)

And again,

The question . . . is whether the Defendants have discharged the burden of establishing the substantial truth of their claim that Irving has falsified the historical record . . . the issue with which I am concerned is Irving's treatment of the available evidence. It is no part of my function to attempt to make findings as to what actually happened during the Nazi regime. The distinction may be a fine one but it is important to bear it in mind.

(*Judgement*, 13.3)

The question is whether 'the available evidence, considered in its totality, would convince any objective and reasonable historian' (*Judgement*, 7.5), that is, whether the evidence would be enough to fit the generic conventions. The judgement compares Irving's work to the conventions of history and finds it wanting. Instead of a 'Bolam test', we could, perhaps rather fancifully, imagine an 'Irving test': a historian is guilty of negligence if he or she has not acted in accordance with a practice or genre requirement accepted as proper by a responsible body of historians skilled in that particular art. Negligent doctors are struck off, no longer doctors. It's worse for negligent historians: they only had the illusion of being historians in the first place. Irving was condemned not because of his relation to the past, which is, as the judge makes clear, beyond the remit of the courts, but because much of his writing wasn't history.

This conclusion also raises an interesting point about Lipstadt's book. Her argument against deniers is that they are not objective and that they are anti-Semitic. However, I have shown that historical 'objectivity' is a myth: historical writing depends on methodology, which in turn relies on the historian's worldview. An anti-Semite worldview will, clearly, produce anti-Semitism. Thus, Lipstadt's arguments show that denial is simply anti-Semitism, which is what she maintained all along. By her own logic, Lipstadt simply didn't need the flawed idea of 'objective' history to make her point. Holocaust denial is not history.

Conclusion: Seeing Denial for What it Is

It's true that anybody can say more or less anything, and the best training in history will not prevent racists and neo-fascists from making their claims. However, in our culture, history is given a great deal of esteem. Whatever the wider reasons for this, the esteem stems in part from the respect for the generic conventions that construct history. It is this esteem that deniers seek for their views and that Irving sought by suing Lipstadt and Penguin. It is this esteem, the credit of being a historian, that Irving was denied. Instead, as I stated at the beginning, he was found to be someone who:

. . . persistently and deliberately misrepresented and manipulated historical evidence . . . portrayed Hitler in an unwarrantedly favourable light, principally in relation to his attitude towards and responsibility for the treatment of the Jews . . . is an active Holocaust denier . . . anti-Semitic and racist and that he associates with right wing extremists who promote neo-Nazism.

(*Judgement*, 13.167)

In the light of this trial, and of the discussion of postmodern questions to history, are there hard and fast rules for determining what is and what isn't history, what is worthy of trust and what we should eschew? Christopher Browning asks and answers:

Is there some scientific or positivist methodology that . . . can say here is where bedrock, indisputable fact lies; here is where transparent, politically motivated falsification begins . . . The archetypal cases seem obvious. But if there is a clear cut method to decide the borderline cases, I do not know it . . . the issue of drawing a border line for an 'invalid' or pseudohistory remains uncomfortably unresolved.[42]

There is not yet, and perhaps could not be, an infallible way of deciding what is history and what isn't. However, simply asserting that 'history should be objective' without exploring what this means (and discovering, as historians do, that it is impossible) or counting on history to 'work' without understanding the processes by which it works is bad counsel. Deniers, too, claim to be 'objective'. By trying to explore the 'software' beneath history, and asking awkward and perhaps threatening questions, thinkers like Hayden White reveal more about what history is. And the more we know this, the easier and clearer it is to see what isn't history, and which arguments are not historical arguments. As Lyotard writes, the 'proof for the reality of gas chambers cannot be adduced if the rules adducing the proof are not respected'.[43] (If deniers believed in being reasonable, of course, they wouldn't be fascists or deniers.) The lack of indisputable answers doesn't mean that we can give up maintaining the rules by which these accounts are written and, perhaps more importantly, constantly checking that those rules themselves still work and, if necessary, renegotiating them.

This is significant because we have a duty to remember the victims of the Nazis, especially those murdered in the 'Final Solution'. But it is important also because Holocaust denial – anti-Semitism – does not just affect historians, or Jews. In an article covering issues raised from the trial, David Cesarani argued that the 'Holocaust is the object of fascination not just because it is a gripping chapter of history, but because it has stunning contemporary relevance'. Citing 'ethnic cleansing' in Europe and the Rwandan genocide, racism, eugenics, the treatment of refugees and biological politics – all issues raised by the Holocaust – he argued that the 'routine violation of human rights . . . inevitably evoke[s] past experiences and call[s] for these to be studied and, with respect for all the crucial variations of scale and character, [is] recalled as a warning'.[44] This warning is particularly serious in relation to the anti-Semitic and racist neo-fascists in contemporary society.

Paul Gilroy begins his study of race and identity by citing the anti-colonialist writer and thinker Franz Fanon (1925–61):

At first thought it may seem strange that the anti-Semite's outlook should be related to that of the Negrophobe. It was my philosophy professor, a native of the Antilles, who recalled the fact to me one day: 'Whenever you hear anyone abuse the

Jews, pay attention, because he is talking about you'. And I found that he was universally right – by which I mean that I was answerable in my body and in my heart for what was done to my brother. Later I realised that he meant, quite simply, an anti-Semite is inevitably anti-Negro.[45]

All these creeds of hate are woven together and denial is one symptom. This link was illustrated yet again in 1999 by David Copeland, the neo-Fascist 'Brixton Bomber', who bombed London's Afro-Caribbean, Asian and gay and lesbian communities. Before he was caught by the police, he had been planning to bomb other minorities, including London's Jewish community. His court case came just after Irving's in the spring of 2000 and was another powerful, distressing echo of the Nazis' hate.

Part of being postmodern is being aware that, as a result of the colonial and post-colonial history of the world, the cultures we inhabit are multi-cultures. Multicultural societies are not those where different cultures are assimilated into a single culture (although wonderful things come from creative mixing of cultures). Rather, it is a culture of respect and negotiation between different traditions. As I have argued, Holocaust deniers hate this multiculture: Irving certainly does (*Judgement*, 9.6). Part of what we, who live and share in this multiculture, have a duty to do is fight this hatred wherever and whenever we find it. Holocaust denial is one of the many fronts in this. In order to fight it, it is important that we understand Holocaust denial clearly for what it is: not bad history, not history at all, but anti-Semitic race-hate thinly camouflaged. David Cesarani points out that 'one quality of the Holocaust is that you can say almost anything about it and sound either profound or provocative'.[46] So, while it is important not to get histrionic about this, it is plain where our responsibilities lie.[47]

Notes

1. The *Judgement* refers to that handed down on Tuesday 11 April 2000 by The Hon. Mr. Justice Gray. At the time of writing, it is available at http://www.guardianunlimited.co.uk/irving and at http://www.nizkor.org/hweb/people/i/irving-david/judgment-00-00.html. It is also available as a book, *The Irving Judgement*, London: Penguin, 2000. It is very accessible and well worth reading.

2. Michael Lee, 'A witness in court', in *Perspective: Journal of the Holocaust Centre*, 2000, vol. 3, no. 2, p. 8.

3. Dan Jacobson, 'The downfall of David Irving', in *Times Literary Supplement*, 21 April 2000, p. 12.

4. Elie Wiesel, *All Rivers Run to the Sea*, London: HarperCollins, 1996, p. 79.

5. Joyce Appleby, Lynn Hunt and Margaret Jacob, *Telling the Truth about History*, London: W. W. Norton and Company, 1994, p. 7.

6. Richard Evans, 'Truth lost in vain views', in *Times Higher Education Supplement*, 12 September 1997, p. 18.

7. Deborah Lipstadt, *Denying the Holocaust: The Growing Assault on Truth and Memory*, London: Penguin, 1994, pp. 18, 19.

8. Gill Seidel argues this in *The Holocaust Denial:*

Antisemitism, Racism and the New Right, Leeds: Beyond the Pale Collective, 1986. Dan Jacobson makes this point, too.

9. Frank Miele, 'Giving the Devil his due: Holocaust revisionism as a test case for free speech and the Sceptical Ethic', in *Skeptic*, 1994, vol. 2, no. 4, pp. 58–70.

10. Lipstadt, *Denying the Holocaust*, p. 28, original italics.

11. Pierre Vidal-Naquet and Limar Yagil, *Holocaust Denial in France*, Tel Aviv Faculty of Humanities, Project for the Study of Anti-Semitism, 1996, p. 14. Pierre Vidal-Naquet also wrote several articles opposing denial, compiled in *Les Assassins de Mémoire*, Paris: Éditions de la Découverte, 1987, a strong influence and precursor to Lipstadt's work. In English as *Assassins of Memory*, trans. Jeffery Mehlman, New York: Columbia University Press, 1993.

12. This is why, with the exception of Irving, I have not named any of the deniers in this book. This is not a book rebutting denial, as there are much better qualified people than me to do that: this is a book about denial, postmodernism and history. The books and articles cited in this bibliography are sources for information on rebutting deniers.

13. Lipstadt, *Denying the Holocaust*, p. 207.

14. Ibid., p. 208.

15. Ibid., p. 208.

16. Peter Novick, *The Holocaust and Collective Memory: The American Experience*, London: Bloomsbury, 2000, p. 271. Published in the USA as *The Holocaust in American Life*.

17. *The Guardian*, 12 April 2000, p. 22.

18. See Robert Jan Van Pelt, *The Science of Holocaust Research and the Art of Holocaust Denial*, Ontario: Department of Geography, University of Waterloo, 1999, p. 17.

19. Lord Lester of Herne Hill, QC, 'Finding a common purpose', in *The Observer*, 23 July 2000, p. 28.

20. Neal Ascherson discusses (and also dismisses) this view in 'The battle may be over – but the war goes on', in *The Observer*, 16 April 2000, p. 19.

21. See, for example, Keith Jenkins, *Rethinking History*, London: Routledge, 1991, for an excellent, highly accessible introduction. See also: Keith Jenkins, *On 'what is history?'*, London: Routledge, 1995, and Keith Jenkins (ed.), *The Postmodern History Reader*, London: Routledge, 1997; Alun Munslow, *Deconstructing History*, London: Routledge, 1997. Hayden White, *Metahistory: The Historical Imagination in Nineteenth Century Europe*, Baltimore: Johns Hopkins University Press, 1973 is the origin of much

of this discussion. For a complete (and useful) contrast see Richard Evans, *In Defence of History*, London: Granta, 1997 and for the classic Rankean statement see Geoffrey Elton, *The Practice of History*, London: Fontana, 1969.

22. Evans, *In Defence of History*, p. 17.

23. David Lowenthal, *The Past is a Different Country*, Cambridge, UK: Cambridge University Press, 1985, p. 218.

24. Christopher Browning, *Ordinary Men: Reserve Police Battalion 101 and the Final Solution*, 2nd edn, London: HarperCollins, 1998, p. 162.

25. Ibid., p. 222.

26. Daniel Jonah Goldhagen, *Hitler's Willing Executioners: Ordinary Germans and the Holocaust*, London: Abacus, 1997, p. 24.

27. Ibid., p. 8.

28. Ibid., p. 21.

29. Ibid., p. 24.

30. Ibid., p. 47.

31. Browning, *Ordinary Men*, p. 191.

32. White, *Metahistory*, p. 2.

33. Ibid., p. 6

34. Frank Kermode, *The Genesis of Secrecy*, London: Harvard University Press, 1979, p. 117.

35. Elton, *The Practice of History*, p. 68.

36. Kermode, *The Genesis of Secrecy*, p. 116.

37. Evans, *In Defence of History*, p. 252.

38. Another excellent discussion of postmodernism and denial, less influenced by Lyotard, is by Patrick Finney, 'Ethics, historical relativism and Holocaust denial', in *Rethinking History*, 1998, vol. 2, no. 3, pp. 359–70.

39. Jean-François Lyotard, *The Differend: Phrases in Dispute*, trans. Georges Van Den Abbeele, Manchester, UK: Manchester University Press, 1988, p. 4.

40. Ibid., p. 50.

41. Ibid., p. 19 (translation slightly modified).

42. Christopher Browning, 'German memory: judicial interrogation, and historical reconstruction: writing perpetrator history from postwar testimony', in Saul Friedlander (ed.), *Probing the Limits of Representation*, London: Harvard University Press, 1992, pp. 33–5.

43. Lyotard, *The Differend*, p. 16.

44. David Cesarani, 'History on trial', in *The Guardian*, 18 January 2000.

45. Paul Gilroy, *Between Camps: Nations, Culture and the Allure of Race*, London: Penguin, 2000.

46. David Cesarani, 'Holocaust on the right side of kitsch', in *Times Higher Education Supplement*, 7 July 2000, p. 20.

Select Bibliography

Joyce Appleby, Lynn Hunt and Margaret Jacob, *Telling the Truth about History*, London: W.W. Norton and Company, 1994.

Neal Ascherson, 'The battle may be over – but the war goes on', in *The Observer*, 16 April 2000, p. 19.

Christopher Browning, *Ordinary Men: Reserve Police Battalion 101 and the Final Solution*, 2nd edn, London: HarperCollins, 1998.

David Cesarani, 'History on trial', in *The Guardian*, 18 January 2000.

David Cesarani, 'Holocaust on the right side of kitsch', in *Times Higher Education Supplement*, 7 July 2000, p. 20.

Geoffrey Elton, *The Practice of History*, London: Fontana, 1969.

Richard Evans, *In Defence of History*, London: Granta, 1997.

Richard Evans, 'Truth lost in vain views', in *Times Higher Education Supplement*, 12 September 1997, p. 18.

Patrick Finney, 'Ethics, historical relativism and Holocaust denial', in *Rethinking History*, 1998, vol. 2, no. 3, pp. 359–70.

Saul Friedlander (ed.), *Probing the Limits of*

Representation: Nazism and the 'Final Solution'. London: Harvard University Press, 1992.

Paul Gilroy, *Between Camps: Nations, Culture and the Allure of Race*, London: Penguin, 2000.

Daniel Jonah Goldhagen, *Hitler's Willing Executioners: Ordinary Germans and the Holocaust*, London: Abacus, 1997.

Keith Jenkins, *On 'What is History?'*, London: Routledge, 1995.

Frank Kermode, *The Genesis of Secrecy: On the Interpretation of Narrative*, London: Harvard University Press, 1979.

Lord Lester of Herne Hill, QC, 'Finding a common purpose', in *The Observer*, 23 July 2000, p. 28.

Deborah Lipstadt, *Denying the Holocaust: The Growing Assault on Truth and Memory*, London: Penguin, 1994.

David Lowenthal, *The Past is a Different Country*, Cambridge, UK: Cambridge University Press, 1985.

Jean-François Lyotard, *The Differend: Phrases in Dispute*, trans. Georges Van Den Abbeele, Manchester, UK: Manchester University Press, 1988.

Frank Miele, 'Giving the Devil his due: Holocaust revisionism as a test case for free speech and the Sceptical Ethic', in *Skeptic*, 1994, vol. 2, no. 4, pp. 58–70.

Peter Novick, *The Holocaust and Collective Memory: The American Experience*, London: Bloomsbury, 2000. Published in US as *The Holocaust in American Life*.

Robert Jan Van Pelt, *The Science of Holocaust Research and the Art of Holocaust Denial*, Ontario: Department of Geography, University of Waterloo, 1999.

Gill Seidel, *The Holocaust Denial: Antisemitism, Racism and the New Right*, Leeds, UK: Beyond the Pale Collective, 1986.

Pierre Vidal-Naquet and Limar Yagil, *Holocaust Denial in France*, Tel Aviv Faculty of Humanities, Project for the Study of Anti-Semitism, 1996.

Pierre Vidal-Naquet, *Les Assassins de Mémoire*, Paris: Éditions de la Découverte, 1987.

Elie Wiesel, *All Rivers Run to the Sea*, London: HarperCollins, 1996.

Hayden White, *Metahistory: The Historical Imagination in Nineteenth Century Europe*, Baltimore: Johns Hopkins University Press, 1973.

Acknowledgements

This book is dedicated to my brother William Eaglestone, with degrees in both Law and History. Thanks also, whether we agree or not, to: Donald Bloxham, Bryan Cheyette, Josh Cohen, Patrick Finney, Lynne Humphrey, Peter Longerich, Jennifer Neville, Jo Reilly, Adam Roberts, Dan Stone, Julian Thomas and all at the Art History and Archaeology Department at Manchester University, and Nadia Valman. Thanks also to all those at Icon Books who have taken such care over this book. All mistakes remain, of course, my own. I am grateful to Royal Holloway, University of London for giving me research leave and to the Leverhulme Trust for giving me a Research Fellowship, and to the Staff at the Wiener Library and the British Library. Most of all, I owe a debt of gratitude to Geraldine Glennon.